KINGFISHER READERS

level 1

Jobs People Do

Thea Feldman

KINGFISHER
NEW YORK

KINGFISHER
LONDON & NEW YORK

Copyright © Macmillan Publishers International Ltd 2012
Published in the United States by Kingfisher,
120 Broadway, New York, NY 10271
Kingfisher is an imprint of Macmillan Children's Books, London.
All rights reserved.

Distributed in the U.S. and Canada by Macmillan,
120 Broadway, New York, NY 10271

Library of Congress Cataloging-in-Publication data
has been applied for.

Series editor: Thea Feldman
Literacy consultant: Ellie Costa, Bank St. College, New York

ISBN: 978-0-7534-6847-0 (HB)
ISBN: 978-0-7534-6845-6 (PB)

Kingfisher books are available for special promotions
and premiums. For details contact: Special Markets
Department, Macmillan, 120 Broadway,
New York, NY 10271.

For more information, please visit
www.kingfisherbooks.com

Printed in China
15 14 13 12
12TR/1019/WKT/UNTD/105MA

Picture credits
The Publisher would like to thank the following for permission to reproduce their material.
Every care has been taken to trace copyright holders.
Top = t; Bottom = b; Center = c; Left = l; Right = r
Cover Photolibrary/Index Stock imagery; Pages 3cl Corbis/Edward Bock; 3cr Shutterstock/Monkey Business
Images; 3bl Corbis/Angel Wynn/Nativestock; 3br Corbis/Kelly-Mooney Photography; 4 Shutterstock/iofoto;
5 Corbis/LWA-Dann Tardif; 6 Shutterstock/Stephen Coburn; 7 Photolibrary/White; 8 Photolibrary/White;
9 Corbis/Richard T. Nowitz; 10 Shutterstock/CandyBoxPhoto; 11 Photolibrary/White; 12 Corbis/Patrick Lane/
Somos Images; 13 Corbis/Ariel Skelley/Blend Images; 14 Shutterstock/OtnaYdur; 15 Corbis/Anderson Ross/
Blend Images; 16 Alamy/Blend Images; 17 Alamy/fStop; 18 Alamy/Steve Skjold; 19 Photolibrary/Cuboimages;
20 Shutterstock/Lars Christiansen; 20b Corbis/Marc Mueller/dpa; 21 Photolibrary/Bios; 22–23 Getty/NASA;
24 Photolibrary/ Index Stock Imagery; 25 Photolibrary/ Index Stock Imagery; 26 Getty/Angel Martinez;
27 Photolibrary/Imagebroker; 28 Shutterstock/Lurii Osadchi; 29 Shutterstock/Igor Bulgarin; 30tr Corbis/
Paul Burns; 30cl Alamy/Blend Images; 30b Shutterstock/Kurhan; 31c Shutterstock/pistolseven;
31b Shutterstock/Denis Sabo.

It is a busy day!

People are working.

They are doing their jobs.

What are some jobs people do?

There are many jobs in your town.

A **teacher** does one job you know.

A teacher helps kids learn many things.

You know the job a **mail carrier** does too.

A mail carrier brings the mail to your home.

This person helps build new homes.

These people help
other people move.

Police officers work
to keep your town safe.

Firefighters put out fires.

They keep the town safe too.

A **doctor** in your town helps
sick people feel better.

This doctor helps
sick animals
feel better!

She is called a **vet**.

There are many jobs in the stores in town too.

A **grocer** sells food for your family to eat at home.

Someone adds up the prices
so your family can pay.

Someone puts the food in bags.

Do you like to eat
in a restaurant?

The cook
is called
a **chef**.

What is this
chef making?

Someone brings
your food.

Yum!

Whose shop do you visit
when you need a haircut?

The hair-cutter's shop!

At the flower shop, someone sells flowers and plants.

A bus driver works in town.

A taxi driver may work in town too.

A taxi driver takes people where they need to go.

A **pilot** flies an airplane.

A pilot's job takes him far from home.

There are more jobs
that happen far from home.

This person studies animals
where the animals live!

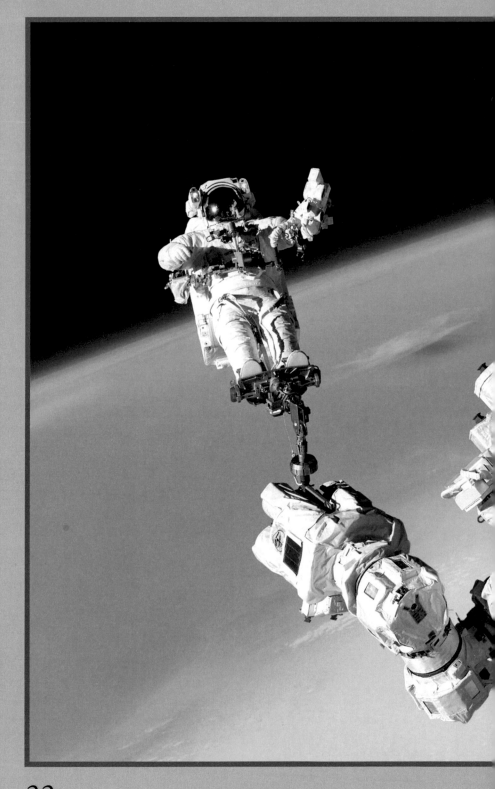

An **astronaut** works
in space to help us
learn about it.

An astronaut's job is
really far from home!

A farmer's job is where he lives.

He lives in a house on a farm.

A farmer may plant food,
such as corn.

He may have cows
and chickens.

Some jobs may not look like work.

But they are!

Soccer players work hard to win a game.

Goal!

A zookeeper feeds the animals at the zoo.

People in a band play music.

They work hard to sound good!

A dancer does her job
on a stage.

There are so many jobs people do.

What do you want to do
when you grow up?

Is it in this book?

Glossary

astronaut someone who works in space

chef someone who cooks in a restaurant

doctor someone who helps sick people get well

firefighters people who put out fires

grocer someone who works in a grocery store

mail carrier someone who delivers the mail

pilot someone who flies an airplane

police officers people who keep your neighborhood safe

teacher someone who helps you learn many things

vet a doctor who helps animals feel better